Investing

Proficiently Mastering The Techniques Of Swing Trading And Investing: Proficiently Mastering The Art Of Price Action Trading

(An Exposition On Dividend Stocks And Achieving Early Retirement)

Bertrand Martinez

TABLE OF CONTENT

Find The Gem In The Rubble

Finding a deal is the best approach to buying a more comfortable home in a more pleasant area. So, how would you find a deal in a highly educated and competitive market?

First of all, there will always be some people who are essentially ignorant of the true value of their home. Furthermore, a vendor will frequently be convinced and require a quick sale. A few examples would include someone going through a separation, losing their job, or moving as part of a task move. These people might just find you to be the solution to their problems. You might get a good deal in exchange if you approach them with a strong offer.

The other incentivized sellers only need to confirm that you intend to follow through on the purchase. Occasionally, the truth that the previous buyer was removed from the agreement is their source of inspiration. You can provide them with a higher-than-usual refundable security store to convince them you are compelled to agree. Additionally, once your inquiry is finished and you receive your credit endorsement letter, you can set aside portions of the security installment, which will no longer be refundable. You can usually receive a good deal if you make a compelling offer to an inspired merchant and convince them you won't back out of the agreement.

Purchasing a light fixer is another strategy for obtaining a reasonably priced property. I'm not discussing large, fundamental issues like materials, establishments, restrooms, or kitchens. I'm trying to locate a gem, just waiting to be found. Many properties don't appear well or don't have a "check claim" because of a small problem. This is often only paint, rug, and finishing. You do not need to complete the task by yourself. You can paint the property with some of your buy credit. The number of high-quality residences that would sell for significantly more money if the seller had painted the ugly rooms would astound you! Instead, examine and paint these features before you move in to save this extra incentive for yourself. A property's latent capacity should be investigated, but you should never pay more than it is currently worth.

Purchase the Worst Property in the Most Affordably Located Neighbourhood

It's a well-known tenet in the land business that you should never own the priciest house in the neighborhood since it won't appreciate much, and whatever more money you invest into it won't guarantee future appreciation. The appraisers cannot locate comparable properties, and the neighborhood will not appeal to anyone looking for a nice home.

On the other hand, buying the worst house in the neighborhood is rather smart. Assuming you follow through on this, modest improvements can raise the home's worth. If you buy a less fancy model or a house with much space for improvement, you will truly desire to improve the property.

Long-Term, Middle-Term, And Short-Term Savings

You should have some cash in reserve before purchasing your first investment property. This will be necessary if you purchase the property from a typical moneylender. They need to be sure you will truly desire to make the house loan installments, even if the property is vacant or has other problems for a few months. However, not every speculative property is acquired via conventional channels. While there are many ways to purchase land without requiring much, or occasionally even any, capital, as I shall look at in Chapter 8, I will never recommend purchasing land without adequate reserves.

Controlled danger is the essence of real home contributing. It is only really as dangerous as you let it be. Suppose you purchase a venture property without money in your bank account, investment funds, or other records. How will you handle the situation where an occupant damages the property, and you need to cover the costs of repairs? This will not only greatly increase the strain, but it may also result in property loss.

"Be ready for the more awful; however, anticipate the best" is a phrase I often employ. I accomplish this by promising to have stored data in a fluid or semi-fluid record for a half-year. I should acknowledge that this was not always the case for me, just like it wasn't for some of the earliest financial donors. I didn't have enough money to enter a half-year's earnings when I started. I hardly had any resources; in fact, my net worth was nothing. I accepted the challenge since, at the moment, I had everything to gain by trying. Although I wasn't prepared to wait a few more years to be able to set away holdings, I wouldn't advise this for everyone. Fortunately, I did have some accessible credit on a few credit cards that I could have utilized for unexpected expenses. Do you think this is you? I could never suggest risking all your hard work on a speculative idea without guaranteeing advancement, but something has to change for me. Even though I didn't need to stop living at this point, I still needed to live it to the fullest!

If you choose to follow the alert route, which is advised, you should start conserving money and attending to your awful duty simultaneously. Starting early and handling some money regularly is the best way to accomplish this. Both your investing account and your financial records should contain some cash. If at all possible, start contributing funds to a shared asset account. You'll be surprised at how quickly these records build if you effectively manage the money each month. An IRA may be included in your shared asset record, which can provide further tax benefits. Some moneylenders would rather not see a retirement account as part of your stores, but you may often convince them that if you fully anticipated taking money out of the record, you could and would. If you start contributing only five percent of your income to the common asset, your stores will grow together with the growth of your venture properties. That's how easy it is!

How Investing Is Affected By Your Credit Score

Your career as a land contributor is greatly impacted by your FICO score. FICO scores for buyers might be as low as 300 or as high as 850. Knowing your FICO score on a regular basis will help you anticipate what kind of finance you are eligible for. For example, you are deemed to have premium credit and will qualify for the best rates and terms if your FICO rating or FICO score is greater than 700. Given your exceptionally high FICO score, you may be eligible for loans with low or no initial installment requirements, such as expressed pay loans.

You are regarded as having excellent to fair credit if your score is in the 600s. Getting high credit-to-value (LTV) advances and using stated pay instead of completing paperwork become a little more difficult. It becomes more and more laborious to fully document your pay when you have several speculation properties because you have to show every aspect of each pay property. To obtain the best wellness rates (more income!), most notable advance-to-esteem proportions, expressed pay sections, complete documentation, and generally more perfect arrangements, you should make every effort to raise and maintain your FICO evaluation.

Chapter 1: Future Prospects, Metaverse, NFTs, and Cryptos

The Metaverse is the next big thing in human history, but this is nothing new. It would completely transform the world as we know it and offer countless opportunities to both current and future generations.

The goal of the Metaverse is to establish a venue where our physical presence at events will no longer be required to participate. We participate digitally, but not in a restricted way, as with the current video conferences and calls. You will be able to attend using the avatar of your choice and engage in virtual property tours, handshakes, and embraces.

The NFTs are just one bizarre aspect of the Metaverse. Now, picture the experience of purchasing avatars. It will resemble purchasing boutique stock jeans.

The Metaverse and gaming industries will provide the blockchain's true utility. Some people only want to play games and interact with their loved ones in the Metaverse; they don't give a damn about the price of coins.

Companies are starting to relocate to online platforms. You won't have to travel in order to accomplish certain goals.

You can order things from the virtual world and have them delivered offline, even though there will always be a connection between the virtual and offline worlds.

Depending on the purchase, you can purchase goods from online stores and use them digitally in the same way.

You can choose to read an eBook in a calm setting after virtually purchasing it. All you have to do is go to the online store of the eBook dealers, purchase the book, choose your preferred live background theme, and start reading. Companies will charge for premium backdrops, or you can use the ones that are available for free. You can do all of these things in your room.

The value is where the money is.

It is possible to create a distinctive virtual game house that draws players from all over the world who ask to pay to enter the virtual game settings and play their games. This will raise the virtual property's worth.

There will be streets and homes with animated virtual inhabitants, along with, of course, advertising signs. To promote your goods on the virtual streets, you can purchase ad spaces.

People are already buying land at lower prices right now to sell to you when you wake up for higher prices.

Remember that the government will also be involved, and you will be required to pay taxes there.

This text is lengthy enough; there is more to this Metaverse. I'll be writing more in-depth pieces about this subject shortly, and yes, we are already developing a blockchain-based product that will eventually take advantage of this Metaverse.

Features that Make Up the Metaverse

The designers of crypto metaverses have frequently tried to set their worlds apart from earlier iterations of metaverses in three vital ways:

Decentralization: Crypto metaverses, in contrast to previous digital environments that were controlled and owned by businesses, are frequently democratic in nature, with all or some of their metaverse gaming components built on the blockchain. Because of this, blockchain-based metaverses seem to depart from the conventional corporate frameworks and value extraction tactics used by the game industry today. Games built on the blockchain have a unique quality that can provide players with more equitable ways to participate. It also suggests that people in the Metaverse have joint ownership of it. The game might continue to function endlessly even in the improbable case that the original creators of the metaverseblockchain decided not to pursue the project.

User Management: Crypto metaverses like Decentraland use governance tokens and DAOs (Decentralised Autonomous Organisations) to give their players control over the game's future by letting them vote on changes and improvements. In this way, metaverses may develop beyond being just games based on cryptocurrencies to become fully-fledged communities with democratic economies and governance.

Verifiable Provenance: In cryptocurrencymetaverses, tokens such as NFTs are utilized as in-world products. In virtual worlds, purchases and accomplishments can hold significant value for gamers. Non-fungible tokens give asset marketplaces the much-needed transparency and accessibility, modernizing in-game product standards. Because each non-fungible token is unique, metaverse coins and other items may be easily coded to assist in authenticating the source of user-guaranteed in-game content as well as non-fungible token gaming resources.

Real Economic Worth: The economics of crypto metaverses are closely related to the broader crypto business because they use cryptocurrency and blockchain technology. Avatar skins, digital properties, and metaverse currencies can now be exchanged for their true value on NFT exchanges and other decentralized exchanges.

How To Stay Off Airbnb's Banned List

With more than 6 million available listings and more than 1 billion reservations made, Airbnb has established itself as the preferred choice for anyone looking to offer a property for short-term rental. There's a risky black side to doing business when a host collaborates with the biggest player in the short terminal game. You have to be prepared to host at your own risk if you decide to offer your property on an Airbnb network. When users violate Airbnb's terms of service, the company has a long history of banning individuals—both hosts and guests—from the platform without providing a reason or notice.

This section will discuss an incident involving a gentleman from the European Union who claimed he was banned without realizing they had broken the terms of service. After doing extensive research, I was able to gather the knowledge I needed to impart to you so you wouldn't run the same risk of being banned. Because they are engaging in the same activity as this host in the EU, many hosts on the

Airbnbnetwork run the risk of facing the same ban.

For context, there are two different kinds of bans. In addition to clearing your calendar and canceling all of your reservations, there are explicit bans that prevent you from logging in and conducting business. These are known as shadowbans. They make it so that your listing receives no views at the listing level. We will discuss how violating Airbnb's terms of service can result in a permanent ban and how to avoid putting yourself in danger.

Upon investigating Airbnb's prohibited practices, I discovered that landlords who terminate renters for unpaid rent would not list their houses on Airbnb while COVID-19 was in effect. Therefore, you are not allowed to host Airbnb guests at that property if you evict a renter for failing to pay rent during COVID-19. In order to stop property theft, provide affordable housing, and avoid exacerbating the housing crisis, Airbnb released a statement.

Is Airbnb going too far, though? Do they exert too much control over the circumstances? Do you believe that

Airbnb is assuming that landlords are avaricious and should do anything they want with their houses, or do you think this is a great step to safeguard the good people of the world from being forced to leave their homes because landlords are only interested in making a quick profit?

Cameras and Monitoring

The first ban relates to technology used for surveillance and cameras. Tangential is distinguished from a video by a humorous fact. Since you could ask her what the weather was, a smart home gadget with Google or Alexa built-in is technically a surveillance device. She must listen to the precise words you use, write them down, and then search the databases using those words. That would have to be stated in your home rules because it is surveillance equipment.

If you own smart gadgets, you must disclose that you have surveillance equipment because your smart home records people in your terms of service or house rules on Airbnb. This now relates more to cameras. Cameras are widely used for the primary purpose of keeping terrible things from happening, which is why they are so popular.

I saw a lot of sex trafficking during the Houston Super Bowl in my past experiences with Airbnb, which was not enjoyable. There was a lot of illegal activity going on, with a lot of sex workers coming and going. After I joined the Corps, I stung the person who was escorting girls to and from the apartment buildings and assigning them to jobs.

There have been a lot of strange incidents; I've had people attempt to squat, attempt to steal, and even succeed in stealing goods from my Airbnb. You may require a camera for a variety of reasons, but you should be aware that there are numerous regulations regarding cameras.

Outside your house, a camera is an option. It's not a major concern, and using a perimeter camera is OK. In apartment buildings, installing a camera outside your unit requires approval from the building management. However, you are not allowed in the hallways. Although there are restrictions on that, you can occasionally use doorbell cameras to ring. However, these cameras just function as pointers and only truly activate when someone interacts with your door.

An internal door camera is activated when an apartment door unexpectedly opens. They have their own set of regulations, which we should discuss as this is how a friend was barred from using them. His front door is the only object in the field of view of the camera he has inside the apartment. It seems secure enough, but these are the guidelines and their applications.

Firstly, neither a bathroom nor a bedroom are permitted to have cameras.

That camera cannot be in the line of sight through an open bathroom or bedroom door, regardless of whether it is pointed at a door. It is against policy to stand in the doorway of an open bathroom and be able to see the camera anywhere. These are the two most evident reasons why it wouldn't be a good idea to install a camera in a very small or open apartment. The same goes for the bedroom.

For the sake of simplicity, let's examine a studio apartment. A studio apartment consists of just a bathroom and a bedroom. It is in the same room as the guest's sleeping quarters, even though it may be oriented to face the front door. Therefore, regardless of how far away the bed is, you cannot have the camera in the bedroom. It is still a bedroom even if there is a kitchen between the front door and the bedroom because neither a wall nor a door separates them.

Furthermore, the rules still apply if you advertise any space as a sleeping area, such as a living room, playroom, media room, etc., and if you advertise a couch that can be used for sleeping or if you have a rollaway bed or an air mattress in that space. Also, you are not allowed to have a camera in that room. Assume you have a front door that leads to a mudroom that is closed off and lacks a door separating it from the kitchen. Since there is no door separating the kitchen from the living room, the layout is still open.

Entering the mudroom's cubbyhole, you must hang left into the living room and right into the kitchen. Since the kitchen, living room, and mudroom are all in one room, that camera is still technically in the same space. As a result, even though you can't see the camera until you navigate a labyrinth of tiny hallway areas to get to it, you now have a camera in a sleeping space if you advertise the couch or the area to be slept in. It remains valid and a breach of Airbnb's terms of service.

Because of this, my friend was temporarily banned for possessing a camera in a sleeping area. The most amazing part of this is that the guest informed the host in advance that they were uncomfortable with the internal camera in their home and asked that it be taken out before their arrival. And he did agree to that, taking down the camera before the visitor showed up. However, it wasn't just that one reservation that turned into an issue. The visitor continued to complain to Airbnb about the existence of the internal camera. Due to his failure to follow Airbnb's privacy policies and his failure to monitor his guests, the company initially suspended his account and began canceling subsequent bookings. They then banned him following the completion of their review.

In light of this new information, the first thing you should do is take down any cameras that might jeopardize your ability to continue hosting guests on Airbnb. You can remove all of your cameras and enter through a different door if you have a mudroom that someone walks into and an enclosed space station-style pod where you enter. Well done, if that's how cool it is. Other than having a camera in the mudroom, everyone is at risk.

Go Into The Simulator

Another recent example is the rock band Muse, who have a deal with Warner Music. They just announced "Muse: Enter the Simulation," an event that is based on the 2019 Muse concert that is being relaunched in virtual reality and three dimensions.

With 3D visual effects added within a virtual stadium, the two-hour uncut presentation presents immersive 360-degree graphics that were first performed at Madrid's Metropolitano stadium.

From Muse and the Paris fashion house Balmain, which was designed by Olivier Rousteing, the creative director. One such item is the resuscitation of frontman Matt Bellamy's jacket, which he wore on stage during the show.

Infrared cameras are used for position-based head tracking with viewers. These cameras read data from several sensors, including the gyroscope.

Regarding virtual reality viewers, which you must wear in order to be "immersed" in the virtual world, there are essentially two varieties: those with a single display and those with multiple displays. The latter are typically fitted with two internal lenses—one for each eye—that are worn on the face and resemble large glasses.

The viewers meant to be used in conjunction with mobile devices, on the other hand, lack internal displays and enable you to integrate the smartphone inside, turning it into the viewer's display. The viewers for PCs, consoles, and those that are independent of other hardware are typically outfitted with two internal displays located directly on the body.

It's important to consider the refresh rate of the visuals when purchasing a VR viewer. A refresh rate higher than 60 Hz is recommended to reduce motion sickness, which is the nauseating sensation caused by movement in a virtual world. When the viewer is worn, it provides the user with stereoscopic vision, which enables them to see the three-dimensional virtual environment's characteristic sensation of depth.

Apart from virtual reality viewers, Among these are, for instance, earbuds that allow the user to hear noises and gloves or controllers that, on the other hand, are used as input devices to do tasks like moving, issuing commands, typing on virtual keyboards, and more— especially in virtual reality video games.

Although they are not yet common, there are VR or cyber suits that surround the entire body to perform a three-dimensional scan and transfer it to the virtual environment.

Virtual reality has many uses because of its versatile characteristics and intriguing qualities. Of course, the first one has to do with video games. In fact, virtual reality makes it possible to experience a high degree of immersion when playing a video game firsthand.

But there are other uses for virtual reality. Consider the educational field, where VR can be used to learn geography, history, art, and a host of other subjects. It gives users the chance to observe people, places, and environments that are remote from them in both space and time. Usually, this use occurs in museums and on college campuses.

For instance, in the workplace, structures can be virtually designed, constructed, and explored before construction ever begins. This allows for the verification of the structures' structural integrity and reduces the possibility of discovering any design flaws.

Surgeons can use this technology to practice the most difficult surgical stages before they actually do the surgery.

And what about the travel and tourism industry? Users can virtually "travel" the world and select where they want to go on their next trip by using virtual reality.

Conversely, travel firms might use virtual reality to showcase a sneak peek of the services they provide to prospective clients.

Nonetheless, in theory, this technique may find application in any industry.

The primary virtual reality systems available right now are listed below. All you need to do to take advantage of this technology's immersive experience is select the viewer from the list below that most closely matches your requirements and purchase it. In comparison to a few years ago, prices are today relatively inexpensive.

With an OLED display that offers a field of vision of more than 90 degrees horizontally and 110 degrees diagonally and a refresh rate of 90 hertz, the Oculus Rift is a viewer. It needs to be linked to the PC.

The PlayStation VR is a headgear that sports a 5.7" OLED screen with a gyroscope and 3-axis accelerometer, as well as a refresh rate of 90–120 Hz. Because it has a Cinema mode, It goes without saying that this must be used in conjunction with a PlayStation 4.

Oculus Go: this viewer promises a smooth experience with its 2560 × 1440 pixel WQHD screen and frame rate of up to 75 Hz. It can be used independently of a computer, gaming system, or smartphone because it is stand-alone.

Gyroscope and video camera are all essential for accurately monitoring the user's movements. It needs to be linked to the computer.

Samsung Gear VR: One of the most well-liked headsets available is from Samsung. It does not have an integrated display, so you will need to place a compatible smartphone inside. It has a viewing angle of 101 degrees. Compatibility of the SM-R324 model with the following devices is complete: Galaxy S8, S8 +, S7, S7 edge, S6 edge +, S6, S6 edge. Samsung's most recent smartphones are compatible with the SM-R325 model.

Google created Daydream View, a viewer that allows you to experience virtual reality at a price that is decidedly aggressive. It needs to be paired with a supported smartphone that doubles as a display, like the Google Pixel or Pixel 2.

The value of the cryptocurrency Dash has increased significantly in recent years, to the point that we can call it an extraordinary success.

Even after starting to trade other types of assets, a lot of brokers choose it, and a lot of them settle on this digital currency.

This is to be expected given its intrinsic properties, which have enabled retailers to purchase to an ever-increasing degree, favoring Dash cryptographic money over other options and taking into account the significantly higher pricing.

It is evident that this also allowed for a general increase in price and market capitalization.

It becomes immediately evident why the Dash Coin has been so successful over time if we also take into account that it is a cryptographic currency that is categorized as "computerised cash" and has an activity that is somewhat similar to that of Bitcoin.

But rather than disregarding the aspects that make this digital money intriguing, we should keep looking into it to find out what it is and how it works—aside from the fact that it might be a fraud!

In contrast to other digital currencies such as Ethereum or Bitcoin, Dash is undoubtedly an unexpected player in the market.

At its core, it can be defined as a stage of development that uses distributed trades in addition to decentralized electronic currency, which is flexible like the real currency we use on a daily basis to travel across nations.

The main idea is that Dash is built on the same code that was previously used for Bitcoins, but it adds new features like security and much faster transactions.

Similar to Bitcoin, Dash is completely open-source and has its own square foundation, complete with wallets and communities.

In contrast to Bitcoin, there is hardly any exchange fee.

As of right now, we can confirm that Dash will, given the current state of affairs, essentially remain a cryptocurrency for the next few years, much like any other digital currency that still exists. It is a coin with a computerized heart, and it will never truly replace cash.

A specific digital currency known by its name, Dash, was once intended to be Darkcoin and XCoin.

It is often an open-source cryptocurrency that uses a shared sort of trade with the goal of being the most "friendly" digital currency for all traders while also being the one that they swap the most of.

Both private and instant interactions are available. Its self-funded and self-managing model enables the scrambling organization to compensate individuals and groups for tasks that add to the network's value.

Dash is the first decentralized independent organization, and one of its peculiarities is its decentralized administration with a financial plan framework.

Dash Coin is described as a digital (and hence non-physical) currency that enables you to transact through an entirely open-source peer-to-peer network very quickly and securely, allowing you to send and receive money at incredibly low costs.

All of this takes place within a completely decentralized organization, which is unavoidably linked to security, confidentiality, and dependability, as we've seen.

Because of its completely decentralized structure, national banks are unable to control or seize control of The Dash, which has nothing to do with the cryptocurrency world.

Giving all merchants the ability to transmit virtually instantaneous installments with the highest level of anonymity around the globe is a very intriguing perspective for Dash users.

Therefore, it is just a very alluring advantage for all dealers who want to start by being involved in the digital currency market directly. Nothing hurts more than a little history. What if we examine this coin?

Darkcoin decided to rebrand itself as Dash on March 25, a year after it was founded. Dash represents the merging of digital and cash today.

After meeting with the person who created Bitcoin, Evan decided to use the cryptocurrency's core technology to create his own cryptography, which he ultimately named Dash.

Regarding its experiences, we should note that the DASH digital currency was sent out two days after it was created. This involved the mining of 1.9 million monetary standards or roughly ¼ of Dash's total offer. Its creator promised it was an error.

Similar to Bitcoins, Dash is also clearly defined as a small virtual currency with an 18 million coin maximum supply. This element suggests that it's possible that most brokers would view it as a haven asset.

Dash currently has 7.4 million units in stock, and it will grow to 18.9 million units out of 2300 units.

Dash also has a variable square compensation, although it decreases to a 7.1% annual rate in any case.

The Dash chain block has a normal square extraction season of 2.5 minutes, which makes Bitcoin considerably faster.

Dash Coin functions very similarly to Bitcoin!

Because of encryption, this digital currency is also entirely decentralized, allowing for the sending and receiving of unknown installments. Dash is a cryptocurrency that operates on a public blockchain, similar to Bitcoin, that records all user exchanges.

Despite this, Dash has the advantage of being much faster at exchanges than Bitcoin.

Experts who have recently conducted research agree that this is one of the primary factors that have caused Dash to be far more valuable to users than Bitcoin.

With the help of Dash, installment payments may be sent far more quickly than they could be with Bitcoins, which now have confusing pricing.

According to Ryan Taylor, head of money at Dash, the currency has seen steady growth in the present day due to the use of digital currency by an increasing number of traders and sophisticated payment providers.

Examiner and blockchain item specialist Chris Burniske of ARK Invest claims that the Dash's evident illiquidity has led to significantly exaggerated price swings.

As a result of carrying out the protective settings, Dash is described as one of the few remaining possibilities, a modified version of Bitcoin.

But this virtual currency differs from Bitcoin in a number of other respects as well, such as how network-wide management decisions are handled.

There are several qualities to Dash that make it unique in its field.

Because of Dash Evolution, which should enable the use of digital money even by those who have no idea what they are or how to exchange them, all Dash allies are also convinced of a bright future.

Neglecting Written Commitments

During the collapse of the housing market, arranging a quick agreement with the dealer's moneylender was one of the best ways to obtain an exceptional arrangement on a home. The bank agrees to acknowledge a sum that is not precisely their complete outcome in a brief agreement. Contract organizations agree to a brief agreement because, in some circumstances, it may end up being better than having to give up the property.

Every borrower has experienced several reports that need to be approved when a house loan is initiated. The bank typically requests certain reports to be agreed upon when endorsing a short trade. A sworn declaration stating that the buyer strikes an agreement to refrain from exchanging the property for ninety days after the purchase date is one of those documents that certain banks need the buyer to sign.

Randy and Roger reviewed the oath the bank required them to sign at the short deal closing, thinking, "What does the bank care and what might they do in any case assuming they discovered that the property was sold in less than 90 days?" Randy and Roger proceeded with their plan to exchange the property to a new buyer for a higher price half a month after it happened because they were convinced that a lien holder for a merchant did not reserve the right to control how another purchaser could manage a resource once they acquired it.

They had to employ two different closing businesses and make sure the new title company was unaware of the affidavits they were signing, which obligated them to hold onto the property for at least ninety days, so it required some serious wrangling to make it happen. Furthermore, they disproved the testimonial commitment by using complex possession structures to alter the person they believed to be the true proprietor.

 And when they'd done it once without any problems, they kept doing it over and over.

The pair had 20 quick transaction closings over the course of two years, exchanging the residences for new buyers in less than 90 days.

However, things began to alter with the 21st arrangement. The fact that Randy and Roger had the choice to swap the house in less than ninety days perplexed the specialist for the new title organization, who had experience with short deals. She contacted the person who had created the document after seeing her name on the deed to inquire about this end, which had occurred roughly a month prior. The former closing expert confirmed what she had suspected—that the bank had made Randy and Roger sign a statement agreeing to keep the property off the market for ninety days. The title specialist graciously informed Randy and Roger that she would not be able to close this until day 91 and that they would be prohibited from trading for ninety days. Unfazed, they looked for a different-end firm that wasn't quite as brilliant.

Due to the limited amount of their upfront payment, the buyers were having trouble obtaining credit in the meantime. Roger and Randy came up with a plan. When closing time came, they would send the buyer the upfront payment in the form of a clerk's cheque drawn on their account, but with the buyer's name on it. Since the money they supplied the buyer would be returned to them, they wouldn't have to spend any money on it.

They closed with another title organization after carrying out the arrangement perfectly. After more than two years of excellent performance, Randy and Roger calculated that they had accrued net benefits of more than

$500,000. They praised themselves and thought of themselves as geniuses for overcoming obstacles that other investors were unable to overcome.

Unfortunately, a few months after closing on the home, the buyers under the 21st agreement began to have financial difficulties. They requested an advance modification because they were having difficulty paying their house loan installments. After going through all of the borrowers' archives in the credit alteration bundle, their home loan company began to notice mistakes with the initial advance application that they had submitted when they bought the house. This was disregarded during further inspections, which also revealed the unusual clerk's cheque at the conclusion that it didn't seem to originate from any of the borrowers' bank accounts.

Through their acceptance of the first payment from dealers Randy and Roger, the borrowers had consented to credit blackmail. However, the bank chose to focus on Randy and Roger rather than these hardworking mortgage holders.

The bank focused on the group that had given the property to the vendors because they had nearly infinite resources to pay for legal investigations, and the investigators soon realized that they might have struck gold. Not only had Randy and Roger planned to submit a contract that was falsely represented by giving the borrowers the first installment when closing time came, but even more seriously, they had signed witness testimony stating that they would not sell the property in less than ninety days, and they had followed through on that promise.

Roger and Randy faced legal action. Rather than engage in an arduous and costly legal battle, both Randy and Roger came clean. They are currently incarcerated and are hoping for a lesser sentence through further work with their attorney.

The Financial Markets And How They Operate

Bonds, currencies, commodities, and stocks make up the financial markets.

Every nation in the world has share markets. It is the London Stock Exchange in the UK and the New York Stock Exchange and Nasdaq in the US.

Commodity markets are places where goods like gold, silver, crude oil, and other agricultural commodities can be bought and sold. While the majority of activity in these markets comes from users transacting for commercial purposes, a sizable portion of individuals and institutions purchase and sell speculatively in an attempt to profit from market price swings. Instead of viewing market swings as their enemy, they see them as their ally.

Currency exchange is possible in currency markets, commonly referred to as forex markets. For instance, an Indian who wishes to travel to the United States will want $, which he can obtain by changing rupees into dollars. Any importer who wishes to purchase items from Japan must pay the exporter in Japan in Yen. In addition to these sincere users, there exist individuals who engage in currency trading with the intention of profiting from the significant fluctuations in exchange rates between various currencies. Forex markets have the highest volume in the world.

Companies and governments can borrow money through the bond market by issuing bonds to the general public and other institutions. In essence, a bond is an interest-bearing debt issued to the government or a business. Bond prices are influenced by a variety of factors, including news, sentiment, economic statistics, and—most importantly—the general interest rates that are in effect in the nation. Bond rates fluctuate in tandem with changes in the nation's bank interest rates. Once more, those who purchase and sell bonds do so in an effort to profit from changes in interest rates.

Any market is a location where people can purchase and sell goods to suit their requirements. Similar markets exist for the purchase and sale of financial goods, including stocks, bonds, currencies, and commodities. For varying reasons, various actors require distinct financial markets. To achieve their commercial needs, certain corporations and other organizations rely on the financial markets. People purchase or sell in order to satisfy their own needs for earnings and savings.

Some people buy with the intention of selling when they receive the desired appreciation. Some purchase with the intention of profiting from short-term price fluctuations in the market. Consider this: perhaps two months later, when prices have increased. The person runs the danger of suffering a loss if the price of gold drops.

Although the reasons underlying the share market's changes are unknown to us, we are all aware of them. In the same way that we witness weather every day, but rarely consider how air mass and clouds combine to create it.

Every day, markets rise and fall in response to supply and demand. In addition to supply and demand, a variety of local and international factors can impact the market price of any currency, commodity, or share. The most influential aspects are those related to the economy, the climate, natural disasters, international politics, international conflicts, and so on. For instance, a conflict in the Middle East may have an impact on several companies worldwide. People might be less inclined to purchase or hold shares of companies impacted by conflict. Currencies and commodities will also be impacted. Rumors have the potential to drastically affect the price of any commodity or share in the near term.

Let me now discuss a crucial aspect of trading, investing, and speculation in these markets and offer my analysis of it.

Throughout my career, the principles of investing, trading, and speculating in various markets have remained mostly unchanged. Let's take a brief look at the principles and various methods of investing.

Section One: Unconventional Knowledge About Investing in Real Estate First Chapter Investing in real estate is unlike any other job.

When compared to other businesses, Those independences bring with them a unique opportunity for compensation. Land contributions make up the majority of the most outstanding financial examples of triumphing over adversity in history. Is it really an industry for you, though?

Choosing any path in life entails accepting the consequences should you choose to follow it. This section looks into a few aspects of the land-contributing industry that you may be familiar with.

There are a gazillion industries in which one can obtain employment. Nowadays, advanced education is available for almost anything. Because of the development of the internet, there are almost no restrictions on the kind of exchanges or organizations you can participate in.

And, like they say, there's something for everyone when it comes to dating.

However, have you observed how the labor market and workplace have evolved over time? Obtaining and retaining employment isn't nearly as easy as it once was. Our ancestors lacked inventiveness, held more serious jobs, and were not frequently employed with professional degrees. After that, the popularity of college degrees increased, making it quite simple for someone to enter the workforce: obtain a degree, and you'll be able to work in that field (probably a 9–5 job). Then, with the arrival of the Millennial generation, it has begun to appear as though college degrees are no longer valuable due to the high unemployment rate among recent graduates. People are now genuinely taking control of their professional paths and earning potential as a result of this.

As things are, occupation security is not guaranteed by adhering to normal procedures.

One of the few businesses that fits this creative inclination is real estate contributing.

Standard operating procedures do not exist for land financial backers. Either a very well-taught foundation or a very little training foundation can produce you. Either wealthy guardians or defenseless guardians can be your exit. Anywhere you need financial support, you can provide it. There is no one correct way to provide financial backing. Your career as a contributor can be anything you want it to be. You truly have the freedom to do anything you choose. What is the number of firms or professions where you can accomplish that?

Being creative while contributing to the land might be seen as either beneficial or detrimental. Some of these qualities will pique your interest in land contributing, and some might even inspire you to go beyond what most people would think is feasible. In essence, they could provide you with a clearer picture of what to anticipate when you enter the realm of land contribution.

You Are the Teacher in Yourself

In the absence of recent changes to the training framework, schools do not demonstrate land contribution. Most of the time, money and cash lack education. I learned how to make parallelograms but not how to accomplish my tasks. Knowing parallelograms isn't always very helpful, I can assure you, especially when it comes to keeping a record of my responsibilities. Therefore, if we failed to learn how to fulfill our responsibilities in school, which everyone must do at some point in their adult lives, we also clearly did not learn the fundamentals of contributing.

This is a major barrier for people who want to start providing land. How are you supposed to work out the solution? Growing up, I was aware of the following non-exclusive information on land contributions: own an investment property, buy a high-rise, flip houses, and recover houses. Each and every bolt and nut. However, I had no idea how the procedure should be used in real life or how to complete any of it effectively. Recall the Orange County rental homes I had a look at. Which one contains the dead rat? How could I have been able to use those to run the numbers? When did I ever learn how to do that, or even that doing so was necessary in order to assess it as an investment? How could I possibly learn what I needed to know in that situation as a novice investor who had no notion of what to look for?

I had to solve it on my own, though. When you first start contributing to the land, you'll most likely be in a similar situation. In addition to learning about the different options available to you as a land financial supporter, you'll also need to figure out how to pursue one of them. It's also going to require you to learn how to do it competently, which is a whole other level, as opposed to just learning how to do it any old way.

In contrast to my earlier experience, TMI currently faces an additional problem: an abundance of data. When I first started, I couldn't find resources to familiarise myself with all of this information. These days, there is so much info available online, thanks to the web, that it may almost be deafening. In any case, how would you determine which info is true and which is pure fiction? Something doesn't become substantial just because it was written online. There's no shortage of get-togethers full of people babbling on about topics they don't really know anything about.

This could make you stop contributing to the land, teach yourself how to do it, and become reliant on whatever strategies you come up with to stay out of trouble. Contributing to land may end up being outside of your normal range of familiarity and outside of your advantage levels, assuming you're not too eager to show yourself new things or you're not confident in your overall drive talents. Contributing land needs a certain kind of drive, which many people lack.

However, if you're like me and enjoy being creative and figuring out how to get things started, you may thrive while presenting the evidence to yourself. There is truly no limit to what you may achieve in land contributing, unlike many other professions where you are taught exactly how to perform things. The land contribution might be great for you if you're free, enjoy learning, have some familiarity with patterns, and are willing to exercise creative, critical thought.

Retirement

Depending on when you retire and how long you live, retirement may last for a significant amount of time or longer.

This is quite important because, generally speaking, the s ate pension will not be sufficient.

You should create a financial plan that accounts for your expected spending in order to determine how much you will need for retirement. Take note that your annuity payment is accessible, just like any other source of income.

Why would you invest money in retirement? In the event that you hope to have a comfortable retirement, you should consider investing in it; otherwise, it will not occur.

When it comes to allocating funds for your retirement, a reasonable balance between risk and reward is essential.

A few of the things you could perform are as follows:

• Put together a comprehensive bring portfolio. A stock and securities list reserve mechanism. The goal is to achieve a respectable long-term rate of return. An annual rate can be extracted. You have the long-term (1 to 20 years) in mind. It is able to maintain a wider spread. To help you with this, you can consult a financial advisor

- Reserves for retirement pay. It's a specific category of shared resource. As a result, our money is distributed among a unique portfolio of bonds and stocks. The endeavors determine how to generate remuneration that is assigned to you on a monthly basis. You are in charge of your money with this kind of endeavor and may access it anytime you choose. Be aware that you will receive less money each month going forward if you remove a piece of your head.

Creating an Isa is an optional way to increase your retirement savings.

One type of ISA that enables you to build up a long-term reserve is a lifetime ISA. Until you turn 60 years old, you won't be able to take cash out of the record without incurring a 25% fee.

 An Isa is the British term for the IRA that Americans are familiar with.

Retirement investment benefits include:
• Not relying just on a state pension.

• Retirement that is more agreeable and joyful; • Not burdening your family

There are no obstacles in your way of preparing for retirement. All you have to do is win.

Step 3: Locate

The most common question I field is, "Where can I purchase an excursion rental?" To be sure, answering this question is a hassle for all accounts. The truth is that each person's experience with the circus tent is unique. There's no one-size-fits-all policy when it comes to regios or types of properties. "What elements drive a beneficial area and property type?" is a better question to ask. Determining the appropriate location and kind of property or your next Lifestyle Asset will be made easier for you if you comprehend the answer to this question.

Generally speaking, I counsel people to start with the potential location of their country estate claim. Avoid overanalyzing things and being anxious about all the questions running through your mind, such as whether it's a small enough area or if it's so crowded that competition seems to be rife. We'll talk about these aspects later, but for now, pick one or two areas where owning a country estate seems like the best option. After that, we'll jump right into the next phases and star removing layers of the onion so you can understand what it takes to be the owner of a lucrative lifestyle asset in that field.

We can tailor our portfolios to our unique needs and interests, which is one of the things I adore most about Lifestyle Assets. Since we both followed a similar diagram, my portfolio will likely look much more unique than yours, but they will both be packed with profitable lifestyle assets.

One of my clients, Ryan, is a busy professional who manages several organizations. When I first met him, his goal seemed to be to enter the short-term vacation rental market. In a 1031 exchange, he was given 45 days to find enough properties to contribute almost $3 million USD.

Ryan has always been successful, and his prior endeavors were also successful. However, he really needed to start investing in homes that excited him, and Lifestyle Assets was the perfect fit. Ryan is often a frameworks and interaction fellow, much like the rest of my customers. Even though he was very financially supportive when he first met me, he wasn't going to take any action until he had made his own decisions and felt comfortable receiving the right kind of answers.

Like a lot of other individuals, Ryan's initial question was, "Where are the most productive regions?" We had to place limits on his hunt standards, which meant we anticipated there to be a predetermined exchange. There are a lot of questions to consider when choosing the right region.

Ryan was under strict time constraints, but he was also quite busy and lacked the energy to work for a short while. We started by identifying the primary areas in which he should focus his family's energies. After doing so, we were able to identify the factors that contribute to advantage in certain areas and types of properties.

Ryan gradually followed the path that had been laid out for him and began to understand the appropriate questions to ask along the way. It also functioned.

Ryan could refine his search, identify advantageous areas nd property kinds, put together his dream team, and purchase five properties across multiple industries that all met his requirements for speculating.

Things To Consider Before Purchasing Call Options

Let's now examine some of the things you should watch out for while purchasing call options. The stock you're interested in should be available for purchase at a price lower than what you anticipate it will rise to. To make sure that the stock price rises above the strike price, you must take this action. Since it's hard to predict the future, some conjecture will inevitably be involved. To make informed predictions about the direction of the stock in the upcoming weeks or months, you'll need to read a lot and conduct extensive study.

Secondly, you will need to factor in the premium's cost in your estimations. Let's say, for simplicity's sake, that you discover a $1 per share call option with a premium. A strike price that is high enough to account for that will be necessary. You will definitely lose money if you choose a stock that is $40 per share with a $1 premium and a $41 strike price until the stock price rises over $41.

Recall that exercising your rights under the options contract won't get you money immediately now. To make money, you'll need to turn around and sell it as soon as possible. Naturally, it's a judgment call to sell as well as to exercise your right to purchase. It's natural to want to hold off on making a purchase until the ideal time, but it's impossible to predict when that will be. Even the most accomplished professionals can make blunders in this situation, which is where trading experience comes in handy. The ideal course of action for a novice would be to exercise your right to purchase the shares and then sell them as soon as the price has risen above the strike price to your advantage and cover the premium. There's always a danger that if you hold out too long, the stock price will begin to decline once more, falling below your strike price and never rising above it until the contract expires.

Accessible Interest

"Open Interest" is one of the metrics you will find when you go online to check the equities you are interested in. This indicates how many derivative contracts are active or open for that specific stock. This value rises by one each time a buyer and seller enter into an options contract. As a trader hoping to profit significantly from call options, you should use open interest to your advantage by searching for equities with significant fluctuations in the number of open trades. It will be important for you to search for rising numbers. This indicates that other traders believe this stock will increase in value soon and are interested in purchasing call options on it.

It goes without saying that you should approach this with knowledge. It will be a waste of time to just go online and search through random stocks; you could have to wait weeks to find anything.

You should monitor the financial news in order to get ready in advance. Read the Wall Street Journal, watch CNBC, watch Fox Business, and peruse any other financial magazines that catch your interest. Learn which stocks the experts are recommending and which ones they believe will move significantly in the upcoming days, weeks, and months. Remember that these individuals and experts are not perfect, so use this simply as a reference. Additionally, you want to stay up to date on corporate news rather than concentrating only on finding stocks that will move. It's important to keep an ear out for news about the creation of new medications or the newest technological advancements. Sometimes, news about that can surface before the stock starts to garner a lot of attention in the markets.

Advice on Purchasing Call Options

A call option with a strike price that you believe the stock cannot beat should not be purchased.

Incorporate the premium pricing into your analysis at all times.

Seek out calls with just enough money on them. These should yield a small profit.

You may be able to get a lower premium on call options that are out of the money. Nevertheless, when considering purchasing a call option, the premium shouldn't be your main concern. In most circumstances, the premium will be insignificant when weighed against the funds needed to purchase the shares and the potential profits if the stock rises over the strike price—that is if the strike price is high enough to account for the premium.

Examine the time value. It is preferable to seek longer contracts if you want to make more money. Recall that in the event that the stock market price surpasses the strike price by the deadline, you will always have the opportunity to purchase the shares at the strike price. The likelihood of such occurring increases with longer time periods. You have more time before the deadline to wait and see if the price rises, even if it briefly rises above the strike price before falling. Keep in mind that you will only lose the premium if it never happens.

Begin modestly. Options trading is not a game for novice traders to win big. That will lead to financial ruin for you. Starting with one contract at a time and building experience as you go is a superior strategy.

The Play Money

Although this buyer may not be a good borrower, he or she does have a sizable amount of cash on hand. It is highly probable that they are novices in real estate investing or have poor credit. Don't throw things away; there may yet be a buyer for those with $3–$5,000 in their bank account.

Keep in mind that you might serve as these people's bank, guiding them to the funds. Just remember that you may set up built-in finance to get the house wholesaled quickly, even if you don't have a whale buying every transaction. We'll walk over how to establish this financing source in a later article, and we'll make sure that your name appears on the cheque.

Watch out for weasels!

You will always run into some purchasers who are unscrupulous, undereducated, or lack sufficient funds while you are wholesaling real estate!

Don't hold it against someone if they don't have a lot of money or haven't done enough study on real estate to make informed decisions. In real estate, we were all probably there at that very moment or are now.

You will find that establishing business relationships with those who have less experience can pay off handsomely. Be a free tutor to these people as much as time permits. In real estate, everything you learn on your own will inevitably come back to you.

Asking the kind of personal questions you'll learn to ask can help you quickly become skilled at spotting weasels. As long as you don't discriminate against anyone based on their race, color, creed, sex, religion, or any other legally protected status, you are free to decide who is eligible for your wholesale deals. You do, however, have the right to choose who has the ability to sabotage your excellent wholesale trade based on rational financial analysis. For this reason, you need as much written confirmation as you can that your buyer will actually complete the transaction and provide you with payment. It's safe to say that this part is essential.

You will surely encounter people whose business ethics are wrong—and perhaps even illegal—as your real estate career progresses. Without a doubt, this is true for almost all kinds of businesses, and the real estate industry is no exception. A contract can be placed on a property by anyone, but not everyone is able to fulfill their end of the bargain.

Here's a quick example of what not to do, taken from the hard knocks learning file. A distributor obtained $500 in earnest money from a buyer on seven separate properties, which was kept by his lawyer. It goes without saying that the wholesaler was expecting a big payout. The investor was well-educated and talked a good game, but the wholesaler didn't do his homework, didn't ask for letters of authorization from banks, and didn't get an earnest money deposit that would have been expected given the terms of the deal (even though these were junker houses). In the end, the investor made no attempt to hide, yet he was unable to seal the deals. He shifted his foot placement. Not only did the wholesaler have to pay $500 in earnest money and title work costs for seven different homes, but he also had to rush to renegotiate and finish the transactions with the sellers.

Had the buyer been pre-qualified, all of these risks and monetary losses could have been avoided with a few more minutes of research. The lesson discovered: Don't take the first bait that's offered to you!

Others might try to take advantage of your wholesale offer. In many cases, this is okay. But you have to verify the legitimacy of the buyer on your own. Tell your middleman that you will honor the agreement and won't exclude him, but first, make sure the final buyer is able to finish the transaction. You can develop the ability to recognize sincere individuals who try their best but fall short of your expectations. Additionally, you will be able to recognize the real weasels that you need to stay away from.

Establishing And Expanding A Company

A lot of folks don't spend the time to figure out what kind of activities will help them go into the zone. They also don't put in the time or effort to develop a plan for expanding and launching a firm. Fifty percent of newly established businesses fail within five years, according to the Small Business Association (SBA). This is far less likely to occur if you are patient and take your time to plan. Your goal should be to start a firm that can turn a profit right away and has a steady stream of clients to support growth.

It's probable that you'll need to expand your clientele by starting small. To expand your customer base and foster goodwill, you must offer genuine value to your clients. Your company needs to be expandable. It must, therefore, be structured in order for it to expand. The prospect of selling your company and receiving a cash payout to "spend each daily in your own way" should not be overlooked. You might set a target to assist you to realise when it's time to accomplish your goal. You'll see in this chapter how others have accomplished this.

First, let's examine Ralph—a man I shall call—and his accomplishments. He was an ordinary kid who performed admirably at school. However, he attended college and managed to cover his tuition, housing, and board, thanks to Pell Grants, student loans, and a part-time job. He was uncertain about his life goals, but he was certain of one thing. Even if it could be done, he had no interest in studying biology or any other science. He was not interested in these topics. He understood that by enrolling in the university's business school, he might avoid those classes. Thus, he acted. He discovered that, while not thinking about his interests or hobbies, he enjoyed the business classes, particularly the finance-related ones. He discovered that he was good at finance and money and that it was something he was interested in. He truly got top grades for the first time in his adult life. He made a important financial decision.

A Sector In Which Ralph Worked With Passion

When Ralph graduated, he began working for a bank. After finishing an internal management training program, he started working as a loan officer in no time. The division to which he was assigned provided loans to construction firms that construct homes, apartments, workplaces, and other structures. Ralph might evaluate a prospectus that these companies would write. It included specifics about their anticipated expenses and the building's anticipated sales price. They also gave details regarding the possible earnings and return on investment.

Ralph picked up building finance rapidly. Ralph also became aware of the potential wealth, and as he was interested in and knowledgeable about finance, he made the decision to enter the building sector. He plotted his course at the library on a few Saturdays and bank holidays, as the previous chapter indicated.

One of those days, Ralph was at the library, sitting in a cubicle listing his assets. It dawned on him that he was a financial guru. He was aware of the costs and the financial aspects of building and construction. He was also aware of the duration required to finish particular stages. He was also aware of the standards banks have to meet in order to approve financing for building. It dawned on him that he was lacking something essential. In addition to having some savings, Ralph had a project in mind for a structure that would help launch his construction company successfully. The issue was that his knowledge of construction was limited. He understood the general idea, but how do you take a drawing by an architect and turn it into a building? He came to the realization that he lacked the contacts required to obtain trades like HVAC, plumbing, and electrical. He was not able to locate the necessary contacts or information.

Was he unable to avoid it?

WHICH WAY SHOULD I GO FOR AN INVESTMENT?

Put day trading out of your mind.

It is not gambling to invest. Therefore, as a novice investor, You may start and close multiple positions in a single day.

Day traders who effectively wager on the differences in movements between pairs of currencies are drawn to the foreign exchange markets or forex. It's also common to day trade bitcoins and commodities. However, you truly need to be an expert in your field. You will lose your money if you do not have expert knowledge and/or sophisticated computer algorithms.

Investing is the process of saving money for the future. This lets the money handle the labor on your behalf. Stock markets climb year after year, even in the rare terrible year. To maximize your capital growth in the financial markets, you can use a number of different tactics. However, you have to develop the habit of looking at things long-term—at least until you've gained some experience.

Put leveraged trading out of your mind.

Trading with leverage involves leveraging both gains and losses. Contracts for Difference, or CFDs, are a useful tool for this. It can be alluring to choose to optimize your gains since you are confident that an asset will appreciate in value. However, you are not a seer of fortunes. The asset's value may also decrease. Furthermore, you will have increased your losses if it does.

Leveraging is frequently provided in 2x, 5x, and 10x ratios.

For instance:

The price of Stock A is $1. You choose to purchase 100 shares at a two-fold gearing. Generally, you do not pay extra for leveraged trades; regardless of leverage, the cost of $100 worth of stocks remains $100.

After that, the price of Stock A increased to $1.10. Due to your 2x leverage, the increase in stock price will benefit you twice as much. Hence, you will gain 2x $0.10 = $0.20 for each Stock A you possess as opposed to gaining $0.10 for each. Fantastic, huh?However, not if the price of Stock A drops by $0.10 to $0.90 per share. Because each share of Stock A you possess will, therefore, be worth $0.20 less.

What is the best way to invest for steady cash flow?

Money flow? If you want to invest in cash flow, your best bet is to invest in property. Then, you can expect a regular influx of income via rent. This is, by far, the most proven investing technique for achieving steady sums of cash flowing in.

Invest in REITs

REITs are Real Estate Investment Trusts. These allow you to obtain exposure to property values without actually owning or selling property.

The beautiful thing about REITs, which are administered by businesses, is that 90% of profits must be paid out in dividends. This means you can be sure of a regular annual income from your investment.

Invest in dividend-paying firms.

On the stock market, your greatest bet for sustained cash flow is to invest in select stocks that offer significant dividends. A dividend is an annual payout to all shareholders in a firm.

The founder of Nest Egg Guru in Hawaii, US, John Robinson, is a guru who enjoys using this approach.

Few businesses distribute large payouts. The corporation decides whether and when to take this action.

The "dividend payout ratio" is the statistic you need to find businesses that pay dividends.

Holding stocks in companies that do pay dividends has the benefit of allowing you to profit from both dividend payments and increases in the underlying value of your investments.

A drawback of a dividend-based investment plan is that some well-known dividend payers struggle to enhance the value of their shares; as a result, although you may receive an annual payout, the underlying stock's value may not rise much. Another drawback is that you can never be certain if a company will choose to provide dividends or not.

Examining the Dividend Aristocrats Index is a wise first step when looking for dividend-paying companies. It's under S&P Indices' purview. It suggests, like other indexes, that you can join a large group of individuals and organizations who are investing in a variety of companies. Investing in multiple companies at once that have paid increasing dividends for 25 years straight is possible with the Dividend Aristocrats Index.

A DIVIDEND: WHAT IS IT?

A dividend is a sum of money that a business pays to each and every shareholder each year. You might be one of them if you have purchased stock in the business. Businesses have the option of paying a dividend or not. While some do so annually, others do not.

Purchase bonds.

An investment with a fixed income is a bond. Since they are issued by reputable companies and sovereign governments, they are low-risk and do not provide exceptional returns. There is very little possibility that you will lose your money unless you invest in "junk bonds."

For $1000, you may purchase a corporate bond from the Treasury. In essence, you are financing the issuer $1000. The issuer will return your principal, or $1,000, to you after a predetermined number of years. They will make "coupon payments," or interest payments, to you in the interim.

You can invest in bond funds as an alternative to buying bonds directly. This implies that you will get monthly payments and that an expert will invest in several bonds on your behalf. The drawback is that you will probably have to reimburse the bond fund management business for management costs.

Although it carries greater risk, commercial real estate is usually more financially lucrative than residential real estate. To determine whether to invest in a business property, you must fully understand what it entails. Office buildings and warehouses are examples of commercial properties, as is anything else utilized for business.

You can make more money if you own commercial real estate as opposed to just residential, which is a bonus. Compared to investing in a residential property, you will make between 6 and 12% more money.

You'll be in the spotlight and have multiple professional ties. It is crucial that you always act in a respectful and professional manner as a result.

Since most businesses close at night, the most crucial thing about commercial properties is that you will be following a schedule. It is imperative that you maintain organization, answer calls, and finish assignments during regular business hours.

Foreclosures: Once you have expertise investing in real estate, one of the finest ways to maximize your income is to invest in foreclosures. If you approach foreclosure investing properly, you will outperform the typical real estate investor and reap substantial profits.

For those who are just starting out, this is not a suitable substitute.

That being said, there are three ways to make money on foreclosures.

You can purchase from a lender, from a seller who is going through foreclosure, or even at an auction.

You have to pay the lender the whole amount owed in order to profit from foreclosures. However, in most cases, you will be able to pay off the mortgage with little equity left in the home, which makes the purchase a bad choice.

If an investor arranges a short sale, they might be able to buy the property for less than what is owed on it.

When this happens, the lender is typically quite happy to part with the asset in exchange for a portion of the money that is owed to them. Your capacity to work out a short sale will set you apart from other real estate investors and lead to higher profits.

Sufficient Income or Plenty of Assets

When you are financially free, it means you don't need to work or devote any additional time or energy to earning money in order to cover your living needs and many of your life's ambitions. These could be one or both of the following resources.

Separate Revenue

You can be financially independent if you own your own business, receive government assistance, or have other sources of consistent income that don't need you to labor. Social Security benefits are paid each month if you are eligible. Regardless of the amount of time you invest, you can get paid if you have grown your firm to the point where you are able to step back from day-to-day operations. Rent is paid to property owners once a month, while property management frequently oversees upkeep and bears the risk of renting to a tenant who fails to make one or more payments.

You are financially free if you make enough money on your own to cover your needs and wants.

Plenty of Resources

Generally speaking, investments in stocks, cash in bank accounts, and valuable property are assets that promote financial freedom. You must first invest in such assets—typically substantial sums of money spread over an extended length of time—in order to employ them in the process of achieving financial freedom. For instance, the majority of financial advisors would advise you that maintaining a consistent 401(K) contribution schedule is essential to your long-term financial security and stability. Many people may find this to be the case if they begin investing early enough (in their 20s, 30s, or even 40s). However, individuals who put off investing until they are fifty years of age or older will not have enough time to benefit from compound interest's power. When accounting for inflation, their contributions will usually not even double.

Building financial independence with assets could present issues. Consider it a delicate balancing act. In order to have enough money to pay your bills when using this strategy to cover your living expenditures and wants, you must sell an asset. If you are unable to sell an asset (real estate, for example) quickly enough to obtain the money prior to the due date of your bill, complications may ensue. One could refer to those in these situations as "cash poor millionaires."

Although the worth of their assets exceeds $1 million, they are unable to access it quickly enough to put it to use.

When you run out of assets to liquidate before you pass away, it could be a much greater issue. In essence, you won't have any money left over to pay your payments if you deplete all of your assets too quickly.

The majority of financially independent households combine the two strategies. They may have their own sources of income, such as social security, a business, or investments in dividend-paying stocks, but they also likely have enough assets in the stock and real estate markets to give them financial security, knowing they have plenty to fall back on in case things get tight.

Life Objectives

Make a note of the total amount of money (income and assets) required to support your desired lifestyle. Indicate the year you want to accomplish your goals as well as whether or not you will need to make payments for them. Your chances of achieving your goals increase with their specificity. Next, work your way back to your current age and set frequent financial milestones. These could be specific monetary savings or newly acquired assets.

Spending Plan

Creating and following a monthly household spending plan is a crucial way to ensure that all expenses are paid on time and that investments and the development of independent income are proceeding as planned. Creating a regular budget helps you stay on top of your financial goals and strengthens your resolve to resist the urge to overspend. Charge cards and consumer loans with high-interest rates pose risks to your efforts to accumulate wealth.

Clear Your Debts and Dues

Compared to credit cards and retail store cards, student loans, mortgages, and other similar loans typically have interest rates significantly lower, posing less of a risk to your financial situation. You might accumulate hundreds of dollars worth of high-interest debt with credit cards. Being deeply in debt for a long time is the exact reverse of being independent. After all, having debt implies duty and even bondage, which runs directly against the notion of financial independence.

Conserve

Prioritize paying yourself. That's what financial experts typically advise. Enroll in the retirement plan offered by your work and utilize the benefit of any matching contributions to the fullest. Having an emergency fund (or an automated transfer from your checking account) that you may use for unforeseen expenses is also a great idea, and it can be deposited automatically by your company. Additionally, for an Individual Retirement Account, think about setting up an automated contribution to a brokerage.

Nevertheless, bear in mind that the recommended amount to save is hotly contested, and under some conditions, the appropriateness of such a fund is even called into doubt.

Put money into

Investing is the most reliable and effective approach to increase your money, hands down. Right now is the perfect moment to conduct your homework and determine which way to start investing—a 401(k) or an IRA. But get going! The most crucial step is that one.

Keep an eye on your credit.

Any interest rate pertaining to credit cards, store cards, auto, truck, home loans, or refinances is influenced by an individual's credit report. It also affects other items like life insurance and auto insurance premiums. The logical conclusion is that an individual who practices risky financial behavior may also drive recklessly and consume excessively. In actuality, those with lower credit scores tend to be more likely to be involved in accidents and file larger claims with their insurance companies than do people with higher credit scores. This is not to say that someone with terrible credit is a bad driver anymore than it is to say that a 23-year-old man who is single is not a bad driver. He is young, unmarried, and male; thus, his monthly premiums will be higher. One of the various risk pools that insurance companies consider when calculating your monthly premium is poor credit.

Bargain

The reason they think it makes them seem cheap is that many Americans are hesitant to haggle over goods and services. Many foreigners would advise Americans to overcome this cultural disadvantage. You might potentially save thousands of dollars annually. Smaller retailers, in particular, are usually amenable to haggling. Good discounts may be obtained by making frequent or large purchases.

Purchasing coins for gaming platforms

As previously stated, in-app purchases on gaming platforms are made with their own currencies. This is just a marketing ploy used to make the true cost of the products you are buying appear lower. The truth is that purchasing coins with the intention of reselling them is a waste of time and money, even though some platforms let you mine for coins by rewarding you for finishing stages or releasing coins after a set amount of playtime. If they can obtain the coins straight from the gaming platform, no one will purchase them from you. If you could obtain them for free—for example, by hacking into someone else's account—and then sell them for the platform's fee or less, that would make sense. Trying to resell coins from gaming platforms makes little sense after that.

seeking to turn a profit right away

It's advisable to adopt a "wait and see" mindset when it comes to cryptocurrencies. The FOREX market is a superior option for anyone seeking to generate quick money. You could be able to make money in this extremely liquid market in a matter of minutes.

Currently, investing in cryptocurrency requires greater endurance. You have an opportunity to make some nice returns in cryptocurrencies if you can wait a few weeks to see where price movement may take you. Because of this "wait and see attitude," you shouldn't invest a lot of money in a single coin unless it's a well-established one like Ethereum, Litecoin, or Bitcoin.

Acquiring as much as possible

Trying to corner a certain market is nearly impossible with the quantity of coins available now. Furthermore, it doesn't really make sense to hoard large quantities of coins, even if they are only pennies on the dollar. Particularly when the supply is in the millions, this is accurate. The basic law of supply and demand explains why it is pointless to try to acquire as much as you can. Attempting to corner a coin with a restricted supply would be logical. You would be better off holding holdings in different coins unless that is the case. This is an illustration of diversification, which can assist you in offsetting potential losses on one coin with winnings on another.

Describe The Meaning Of An Investment.

The laws of investment are beyond the comprehension of many people. They frequently fail because of this. It is common knowledge that breaking the rules will not allow you to win. To prevent breaching the rules, you need to be aware of them. People who don't know the regulations are another reason why they don't invest. It is essential to comprehend what investment entails. An investment is what? An asset that generates revenue is an investment. Every word in the definition is important to pay attention to. They are essential to comprehending what investing really entails.

The definition above lists two essential qualities of an investment. Any item, asset, or property must fulfill these requirements in order to be qualified as an investment. If it doesn't fit these requirements, it won't be regarded as an investment. The primary attribute of an investment is its value. This indicates that it is a highly significant or practical item. Consequently, nothing you own— whether it is real estate, personal belongings, or other—can be considered an investment. Any item, property, or possession that is useless, inconsequential, or unimportant in any other way is considered an investment. Every investment has a value that can be measured in money. This implies that there is a monetary value to each investment.

An investment ought to have the ability to generate revenue. The second quality is this. It ought to generate revenue for its owner or assist them in doing so. Every investment has the potential to generate riches. It also serves a purpose and has responsibility and obligation. This is a quality that every investment must have. The fact that a possession, item, or piece of property cannot bring in money for its owner or assist them in doing so is an inherent feature of investment. Regardless of price or value, any item that does not serve any of these financial purposes is not regarded as an investment.

This brings us to another aspect of investing that you should be mindful of. This will assist you in judging the value of an investment. Savings money is achieved through investments that do not provide revenue or cash in the conventional sense. The owner may be able to save money on costs by making this investment instead of having to pay for them otherwise. It might not be able to generate any more revenue, though. The owner receives income from the investment, but not always in the conventional sense. The owner or investor can still profit from the investment.

Each and every valuable needs to be able to make money or save money. It must also fulfill the requirements for importance and usefulness in order to be classified as an investment. The second facet of an investment specifically its ability to generate revenue. Based on the observation that most people only take the first aspect into account when determining what an investment is, this argument is made. Most individuals see an investment to be something worthwhile despite the fact that they may reduce income. Long-term, this misperception may have detrimental financial effects. These folks commit expensive financial mistakes that can result in significant losses in the future.

The fact that it is recognized in academia could be the cause of this misperception. In financial studies at academic institutions and publications, assets, also referred to as investments, are jewels or property. Even when they don't produce revenue, businesses nonetheless view all of their assets, including their properties and jewels, as assets. People who are well-versed in finance are unable to embrace this idea of investing. It is inaccurate as well as deceitful and misleading. Erroneously, some organizations consider their obligations to be assets. For this reason, a lot of people view their liabilities as assets or investments.

Many people wrongly view the goods they consume as investments, especially those with poor financial literacy. These people's investment portfolios list the assets that generate their income. It is the financially uneducated who do this. Their financial futures are hopeless. What financially competent people refer to as income-consuming assets are viewed as investments by those who lack financial literacy. This indicates a distinction between those who are financially literate and those who are not. Those who lack financial literacy do not have a future; those who do do.

"How valuable are the assets you wish to acquire with your investment money?" should be your first consideration when making an investment. If everything else is equal, it will be better with a larger investment (albeit it will probably cost more). "How much income can it generate for me?" is the second question. It needs to be a profitable and worthwhile investment. Investing is not what it is if you cannot answer both of these questions. You cannot classify what you are purchasing as an investment. Maybe all you're doing is adding to your risk.